ideals® EASTER

JANUARY 2004

Dedicated to a celebration—through poetry and prose—of the American ideals of faith in God, loyalty to country, and love of family.

Spring sang to me a melody that lingered on the hills, that seeped into the valley like mist from waterfalls.—Geneva Davies

In This Issue

Vol 61, No. 1 January 2004 IDEALS (ISSN 0019-137X, USPS 256-240) is published six times a year: January, March, May, July, September, and November by IDEALS PUBLICATIONS, a division of Guideposts, 39 Seminary Hill Road, Carmel, NY 10512. Copyright © 2004 by IDEALS PUBLICATIONS, a division of Guideposts. All rights reserved. The cover and entire contents of IDEALS are fully protected by copyright and must not be reproduced in any manner whatsoever. Title IDEALS registered U.S. Patent Office. Printed and bound in USA by Quebecor Printing. Printed on Weyerhaeuser Husky. The paper used in this publication meets the minimum requirements of American National Standard for Information Sciences—Permanence of Paper for Printed Library Materials, ANSI Z39.48-1984. Periodicals postage paid at Carmel, New York, and additional mailing offices. POSTMASTER: Send address changes to Ideals, 39 Seminary Hill Road, Carmel, NY 10512. For subscription or customer service questions, contact Ideals Publications, a division of Guideposts, 39 Seminary Hill Road, Carmel, NY 10512. Fax 845-228-2115. Reader Preference Service: We occasionally make our mailing lists available to other companies whose products or services might interest you. If you prefer not to be included, please write to Ideals Customer Service.

ISBN 0-8249-1230-6 GST 893989236

Visit the *Ideals* website at www.idealsbooks.com

Cover photograph: Two early daffodils brave the last snow of winter in a photograph by William H. Johnson.

Inside front cover: The classic shape and deep hues of spring tulips are delicately displayed in TULIPS AND MCCOY, by artist Mary Kay Krell. Photograph by Steve Beasley.

Inside back cover: Three happy children play with a very patient dog in a painting by Agnes Gardner King entitled SPRING DECORATIONS. Fine Art Photographic Library Ltd./Private Collection.

In March

Pat Winfield Young

I can't conceive of anything
Lovelier to know
Than that a robin's gentle foot
Has tracked the clean white snow.

Perennial Optimist

Emily Sargent Councilman

The woodchuck saw his shadow;
The weatherman says "snow";
But I know winter will not stay.
I heard a robin sing today,
And I have trusted robins
Since many springs ago.

Spring Magic
Gene Scott

Deep in darkened woods,
Where dawn comes late on moist mornings
While soft mists rise and fade,
Marigold and hepatica faces fill out
In little families along the marsh bank
And in the lingering shade.

In the stillness no footfalls yet break
The morning calm or stir the creatures
From nests and burrows peeping.
Dew-frosted leaves on the forest floor,
All turned up now and twisted,
Have stayed the winter sleeping.

Above, a chorus of chitters and chirps
Announces the day's first flights
Of sparrows, finches, redbreasts.
Slowly, silently below begin
The crawls and creeps of critters
Searching for their breakfasts.

Bold sunlight beams through the trees,
Across the streams and meadows,
Joining the joyous celebration.
Once again to every living thing
The Master's magic reappears,
Renewing His creation.

Be Like the Bird
Victor Hugo

Be like the bird who,
Halting in his flight
On limb too slight,
Feels it give way beneath him
Yet sings,
Knowing he hath wings.

Previous pages: Apple blossoms are encased in spring ice and covered with snow. Photograph by William H. Johnson.

Right: Dainty pasqueflowers herald the coming of spring in Sauk County, Wisconsin. Photograph by Darryl R. Beers.

No one could resist the invitation to explore these beautiful woods. THE BLUEBELL WOOD *by Alfred de Breanski (1852–1928). Fine Art Photographic Library Ltd., London.*

COUNTRY CHRONICLE

Lansing Christman

SPRING'S LOVE SONGS

The birds will sing my songs of love this spring. I hear their songs from the dooryard, floating to me from the pastel orchards; and, as I walk through the greening pastures and fields, they greet me. In the damp woods and swampland thickets, they take my thoughts away from the chill of winter's last gasp and encourage me to

An American goldfinch pauses on a hawthorn branch.
Photograph by Daniel E. Dempster.

smile at the coming of new possibilities.

There are songs for every occasion: the busy songs that span the hours from dawn to noon and then leisurely ones from noon through the afternoon. The twilight greetings and the lonesome songs of the night also have their special messages. Even though they are not necessarily meant for us humans, these songs bring a unique beauty to the lives of those who take the time to listen.

The warble of the bluebird is a song of love, as is the carol of the robin. The mourning dove's *coo*, as plaintive as it is, is still another, less gaudy love song. The finches, the chickadees, and the cardinals perform their clear notes with such sincerity that we are reminded of the pleasures of truth and honesty in communication. And when the field sparrow announces vespers, I remember the wisdom of Emily Dickinson, who recognized that touch of eternity in the natural world.

The hermit's flutelike call and the *ee-o-lays* of the wood thrush ring down the curtain as darkness slips its arms around the hills at the close of this fresh spring day.

I wish that I could assemble into one great chorus all of these singers and blend spring with love, all in one spectacular performance. What a chorus to tune our hearts to the rhythm of joy! All of these birdsongs are filled with sunshine and stars, joy and ecstasy. Such magnificence renews our hearts and reminds us that the best love song, like love itself, is the most natural.

The author of four books, Lansing Christman has contributed to Ideals *for more than thirty years. Mr. Christman has also been published in several American, international, and Braille anthologies. He lives in rural South Carolina.*

Pink and red tulips contrast with a rustic barn and tools.
Photograph by H. Abernathy/H. Armstrong Roberts.

READERS' REFLECTIONS

Readers are invited to submit original poetry for possible publication in future issues of IDEALS. Please send typed copies only; manuscripts will not be returned. Writers receive payment for each published submission. Send material to Readers' Reflections, Ideals Publications, 535 Metroplex Drive, Suite 250, Nashville, Tennessee 37211.

The Storm

Jane B. Arata
Fort Wayne, Indiana

Beyond the door I saw a light.
It was forsythia blooming bright;
I turned my head to look away
And wished for such a sunny day.

For pregnant clouds, engorged with rain,
Had cast a shadow on the plain;
While through the air winged birds in flight
Answered in the fading light.

But soon their chirping filled the trees
To mingle with the trembling leaves,
As from the heavens burst the rain
And splashed upon my windowpane.

A blade of lightning pierced the sky
And waves of thunder rumbled high;

I pressed my face against the glass
And waited for the storm to pass.

Then suddenly I saw a flower
That raised its head to greet the shower;
Its cheerful bent was sweetly plain,
To quench its thirst on falling rain.

I watched the blossom drink its fill;
And while I waited, ever still,
The raging storm at last was done,
And parting clouds revealed the sun.

I flung my window open wide
To let the rain-washed air inside,
And once again forsythia's light
Burst upon my eager sight.

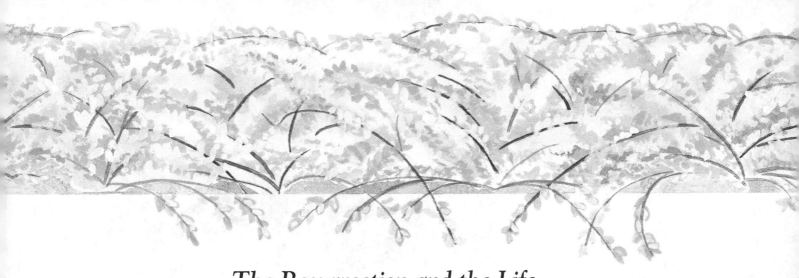

The Resurrection and the Life

Edith Shaw Butler
Bernardston, Massachusetts

And now the crocus breaks the sod,
And now the bird gives voice to song,
Confirming human faith in God
Beyond the winter season long.

For after sleep there comes this hour
To fill the heart with certainty;
From earth's dark tomb there sprang a flower,
The faith that rose from Calvary.

Easter Meditation

Beth Guye Kittle
Elkins, West Virginia

One day when Spring had touched
    the hills with green,
And flowers bloomed
    where April's feet had trod,
They took our Lord
    and nailed Him to a tree.
They crucified the blessed Lamb of God.

Surely the birds stopped
    singing in the trees,
Surely the breezes
    ceased their lullaby;
Or did all nature have abiding faith
That He would rise again
    and could not die?

Was it a day like this—
    of quiet peace,
With pale blue skies
    and white clouds drifting through—
When in His agony
    He spoke the words,
"Forgive them, for they
    know not what they do"?

And now as Spring walks
    softly through the land
And strews bright flowers in the barren way,
We find within our hearts
    this glorious truth:
Our Lord is risen this Easter day!

Easter Snow

Della Susko

Softly it comes down,
Gently covering all the ground
Through the quiet night,
Making a world of white.

There is just a slight chill,
And the air is very still.
People gather in the dark
For Easter service in the park.

At the greeting of the dawn,
Silently snow falls on.

Suddenly the sun peers over hill,
Driving away the morning chill.

Clouds disappear and snow stops, too,
As the sun comes shining through,
Revealing a world, clean and white,
Sparkling in the early light.

There is a new song to sing;
Voices through the clear air ring,
For every heart does surely know
New life awaits under Easter snow.

A Spring Wish

Willene H. Nusbaum

Remembering,
   the martins came back
   to their old home today.
So may beauty forever
   return to you
   on soft purple wings.

Spring Gold

Catherine Donalson

Bright forsythia, goddess of spring,
Survives the winter, her laurels to bring.
Subdued and dormant she waits through the year,
Seeking no favors, demanding no care.
At first sign of spring she stirs in her bed,
Abandons her sleep, and raises her head.
Quite suddenly then her blossoms appear;
Bright yellow spirals are seen everywhere.
Golden, breathtaking, defying the sun,
Her sovereign beauty delights everyone.
Dear lovely flower, so faithful and bold,
You are a treasure of pure, vibrant gold.

*Early forsythia blooms brighten the West Cornwall Covered Bridge in West
Cornwall, Connecticut. The bridge spans the Housatonic River and is still
in use. Photograph by William H. Johnson.*

Morning Dew
Eliot Porter

There is everywhere
dew on the cobwebs,
little gossamer veils or scarves
as big as your hand,
dropped from the fairy shoulders
that danced on the grass
the past night.

April
Sara Teasdale

The roofs are shining from the rain,
  The sparrows twitter as they fly,
And with a windy April grace
  The little clouds go by.

Yet the backyards are bare and brown,
  With only one unchanging tree
I could not be so sure of spring
  Save that it sings in me.

Dew Drops
Helen Prodoehl

Crystal dewdrops hang from branches
Of the April-showered tree,
Where the budding little leaflets
Move like waves upon the sea;
And the moon sends piercing arrows
With its golden shafts of light,
Spraying trees, so crystal dewdrops
Glow like diamonds in the night.

Above: A single tulip is washed by early morning dew.
Photograph by Jessie Walker.

Tulips peep through dew-laden ground cover.
Photograph by Jessie Walker.

FAMILY RECIPES

Pink Lemonade Pie

Anne Sherman, Orangeburg, South Carolina

1 8-ounce package cream cheese, softened
1 14-ounce can sweetened condensed milk
1 6-ounce can frozen pink lemonade
   concentrate, thawed
   Red food coloring, as desired

1 4-ounce container frozen non-dairy
   whipped topping, thawed
1 9-inch prepared pastry shell
1/2 cup shredded coconut, tinted pink,
   optional

In large mixing bowl, beat softened cream cheese until fluffy; gradually stir in condensed milk. Slowly stir in lemonade concentrate. Add a few drops of red food coloring (optional) and stir for desired pink tint. Fold in whipped topping. Pour into prepared pastry shell. Chill until set. Refrigerate until ready to serve. Sprinkle with coconut. Makes 6 to 8 servings.

Daffodil Salad

Ann Katzer, Cougar, Washington

1 3-ounce package lemon gelatin
1 3-ounce package lime gelatin
4 bananas, sliced
1 16-ounce can pineapple tidbits
   (drain and reserve juice)

1 1/2 cups pineapple juice
1 egg, slightly beaten
2 tablespoons all-purpose flour
2 cups miniature marshmallows
1 cup finely shredded coconut, optional

In a large bowl, combine lemon and lime gelatin; follow directions on package to make. Once gelatin has thickened, stir in bananas and pineapple. Pour into a 9-by-13-inch pan and chill until set. In a small non-stick saucepan, combine pineapple juice and egg; whisk in flour. Heat over medium temperature, stirring constantly, until thickened. Add marshmallows and stir until melted and mixture is smooth and creamy. Remove from heat and allow to cool. Spoon marshmallow topping over gelatin; sprinkle with coconut. Chill until serving. Makes 16 servings.

Crisp Pastel Cookies

Judith Herbster, Savannah, Georgia

2 1/2 cups all-purpose flour
1 teaspoon baking powder
1 teaspoon salt
1/4 cup shortening
1/2 cup butter or margarine, softened
1/2 cup sugar
1 3-ounce package lemon-flavored gelatin
1 teaspoon vanilla
2 eggs, beaten

Preheat oven to 400°F. Sift together flour, baking powder, and salt. Set aside. In a large bowl, cream together shortening and butter. Add sugar and gelatin; cream until fluffy. Stir in vanilla and eggs, mixing well. Slowly add flour mixture, mixing well after each addition. Shape dough into 1-inch balls and place 3 inches apart onto ungreased cookie sheet. Flatten balls with bottom of a small glass dipped in sugar. Bake 6 minutes or until edges are firm and slightly golden. Cool on cookie sheet for 1 minute. Remove to a wire rack and cool completely. Store in airtight container. Makes approximately 4 dozen cookies.

Lime Jello Cake

Patricia P. Cox, Memphis, Tennessee

1 3-ounce package lime gelatin
1 box deluxe lemon cake mix
4 eggs, slightly beaten
3/4 cup vegetable oil
1/2 cup fresh lemon juice
1 1-pound box powdered sugar

Preheat oven to 325°F. In a small bowl, stir gelatin into 3/4 cup boiling water, stirring until completely dissolved. Set aside. In a large bowl, combine cake mix, eggs, and oil; mix well. Stir in gelatin mixture. Pour into a greased bundt pan and bake for 1 hour or until toothpick inserted into cake comes out clean. In a medium bowl, whisk lemon juice into powdered sugar until smooth and creamy. When cake is done, turn off oven and remove cake. With a fork, poke holes into the cake. Drizzle lemon-sugar glaze over cake and return cake to the warm oven for 10 minutes. Remove; cool in pan on a wire rack. Invert cooled cake on a cake plate. Makes 15 servings.

Lemons and limes lend their lovely colors to springtime desserts for your family and friends. We would love to try your favorite recipe too. Send a typed copy to Ideals Publications, 535 Metroplex Drive, Suite 250, Nashville, Tennessee 37211. Payment will be provided for each recipe published.

Forests are the ornaments of the earth.
—Anton Chekhov, *Uncle Vanya*

Small Creatures and Ordinary Places

Allen M. Young

What is truly marvelous about spring—oft noted only in passing, as a cliché, and rarely comprehended much further—is that nature's awesome tapestry is woven together once again as if the whole woods is one super-organism coming out of a deep sleep.

Spring, however, can be very different one year to the next. Like a petulant child, the season thrives on inherent unpredictability and guile. In some years, it arrives "early" and in others, "late." Sometimes its display is gradual and muffled, a stretched unfolding of freshened new life sliding to a snail's pace into summer. At other times it is a thin and rushed but glorious and vibrant ribbon whisked from winter's grasp and flung into sum-

mer. Such capriciousness aside, spring's personality is always an elegant symphony, orchestrated stanzas of things being born, shaped, and blended by weather and each other.

Only inside the woods, when meandering toward the flooded center of this place, can we truly begin to sense the ancient seasonal cycle of birth, growth, harvest, and death that has needled philosophers and others for centuries.

This can be the very best of therapy. You reawaken, become restored, as the land around you wakes up and changes its guise. Wisdom is seldom a store of facts. Wisdom seldom comes from books and well-meaning teachers. Wisdom can come from seasoned insights hidden in the land.

Roaring Fork Creek ambles through Great Smoky Mountains National Park in Tennessee. Photograph by Daniel E. Dempster.

Song to a Tree

Edwin Markham

Give me the dance of your boughs, O Tree,
Whenever the wild wind blows;
And when the wind is gone, give me
Your beautiful repose.

How easily your greatness swings
To meet the changing hours;
I, too, would mount upon your wings,
And rest upon your powers.

In the company of flowers we know happiness.
In the company of trees we are able to "think"—
they foster meditation. . . . There is nowhere on
earth we can think so well as in a thin wood
resting against a tree. —John Stewart Collis

*Dogwoods in bloom provide a breathtaking spring scene in Audubon Park,
Louisville, Kentucky. Photograph by Daniel E. Dempster.*

Inset: Detail of dogwood blossoms. Photograph by Daniel E. Dempster.

*Overleaf: A quiet spring scene at Shore Acres State Park, Oregon, invites visitors.
Photograph by Dennis Frates.*

That I May Live
Faith H. Mikita

O my Lord, was Thy sacred head
With thorns pierced for me?
If so, pour Thy blessing on my head,
That I may think for Thee.

O my Lord, were Thy sacred hands
With nails pierced for me?
If so, shed Thy blessing on my hands,
That I may work for Thee.

O my Lord, were Thy sacred feet
With nails pierced for me?
If so, pour forth Thy blessing on my feet,
That I may follow Thee.

O my Lord, was Thy sacred heart
With spear pierced for me?
If so, send forth Thy Spirit into my heart,
That I may live for Thee.

Gifts of Silence
Laurence Binyon

No sound in all the mountains, all the sky!
Yet hush! One delicate sound, minutely clear,
Makes the immense silence draw more near—
Some secret ripple of running water, shy
As a delight that hides from alien eye.
The encircling of the mountains seems an ear
Only for this; the still clouds hang on to hear
All music in a sound small as a sigh.

Far below, rises to the horizon rim
The silent sea. Above, those gray clouds pile;
But through them, trembling, escape—like bloom,
Like buds of beams, for sleepy mile on mile—
Wellings of light, as if Heaven had not room
For the hidden glory, and must overbrim.

Beneath the peaks of Mount McGown in Idaho, Rydberg's penstemons fill a field with spring beauty. Photograph by Terry Donnelly.

23

At Easter Sunrise

Inez Franck

The church bells chime that He is risen
As sunrise lights the eastern sky;
The bells resound with nature's music
As worshipers are thronging by.

The Cross is held with holy triumph
That vanquishes the veil of death.
The lily opens like a symbol;
And wonder's in dawn's new breath.

From leaf and branch, from stream and valley,
A splendor greets the Easter Day.
Around the world each heart is singing
One joy—the stone is rolled away.

Easter Theme

Mary E. McCullough

O happy world today, if we could know
The message of that morning long ago!
There is no dark despair that cannot be
Evicted from the heart's Gethsemane;
For faith is always more than unbelief,
And vibrant courage triumphs over grief.

*Daisies welcome the dawn at Fort Point Cove, Cape Jellison,
Stockton Springs, in Maine. Photograph by William H. Johnson.*

The Chapel
William Daniel Miller

Reaching out to touch the door of
    Timothy and Titus,
My heart slowed and my spirit kneeled
    before the King of Heaven.
Such was my state of mind that
    Earth's magnetic core seemed to shift,
Beyond that stone arc; this new gravity
    pulled my bones into the deep.

My fingers touched lightly because I feared
    a loud shout should shake the place,
    as I dared to go behind the veil.
But You, Lord, have torn the veil at Calvary,
    and so this great door, and this mystery,
    was found unlocked to my entry.

The darkness of the Holy and the heat of
    the morning sun in those great steel doors
Ushered me into a space where the light
    was transformed through stained glass,
Falling softly on the altar beyond Jordan
    where the Son of Man was lifted up.

Crucifying
John Donne

By miracles exceeding power of man,
He faith in some, envy in some begat,
For, what weake spirits admire, ambitious hate:
In both affections many to Him ran,
But Oh! the worst are most, they will and can,
Alas, and do, unto the immaculate,
Whose creature Fate is, now prescribe a Fate,
Measuring selfe-life's infinity to a span,
Nay to an inch. Loe, where condemned He
Bears His own cross, with pain, yet by and by
When it bears Him, He must bear more and die;
Now Thou art lifted up, draw me to Thee,
And at Thy death giving such liberal dole,
Moist, with one drop of Thy blood, my dry soule.

A field of dandelions surrounds a country church in Wonalancet, New Hampshire. Photograph by William H. Johnson.

DEVOTIONS FROM THE HEART

Pamela Kennedy

Sing to the Lord, praise his name; proclaim his salvation day after day. Declare his glory among the nations, his marvelous deeds among all peoples. —Psalm 96:2–3

SINGING A NEW SONG

The choir director cut us off after the chorus . . . again. She sighed and stared at her music for a moment, then looked up and said, "OK, let's take a ten-minute break. Get some water, walk around, get some fresh air, then come back and let's try this one more time."

We could sense her discouragement. To be truthful, we were all discouraged. The church choir contained about twenty folks of varying ages, talents, and devotion to music. Some were in the "make a joyful noise" category. A few had some professional training. Most of us just enjoyed singing. It was early April, and Easter was bearing down on us like a runaway locomotive. The closer it came, the more we felt there was going to be a terrible train wreck!

The tenors couldn't get their harmony line together. The altos overwhelmed the other sections with both enthusiasm and volume. There were some uncontrolled trillers among the sopranos and the bassos fluctuated between booming and absolute silence. With just a week to go, panic was setting in.

We regrouped after the break, freshly determined to get our alleluias organized and on-key.

The director raised her arms, nodded to the organist, and we began. We made it through a difficult modulation with success and the choir director smiled a bit. The bassos held down their *profundos* and the shy tenors gained enough courage to attack their harmony line with solidarity. Then came the *a cappella* section. We sang with enthusiasm, every note increasing in vol-

---

Dear Father, help me approach each day with an Easter hope, determined to sing a new song for You.

---

ume and intensity, enunciating with clarity, ending on one strong, unison note. Then the organ echoed our voices with a triumphant chord—and revealed we were a full tone flat. The director's face reddened with frustration at the echoing dissonance. "Well, that could wake the dead!" she announced.

Initially tempted to suggest that was an appropriate response for an Easter piece, I quickly thought better of it.

Frustration stalked the next few rehearsals. We conquered one part, only to mess up on

The steeple of Ephraim Moravian Church, Door County, Wisconsin, reaches for the sky. Photograph by Darryl R. Beers.

right intertwined beautifully. Each section seemed inspired by the others. We were together, a choir in the truest sense, and, when we hit the final note, the music hung in the air for a moment, floating over the congregation like an offering. In the end, at the final hour, it all came together.

I suspect our musical experience is not really unique. All across the country choirs struggle through compositions that seem impossible, under directors who must feel they should have chosen another calling. But in the end, when their efforts are offered up, God makes something beautiful of the anticipated failure. And isn't that what Easter is all about? After the disaster of Good Friday, the despair of a Sabbath in the tomb, who would have expected a new song of triumph? But the fear and failure experienced only days earlier turned to joy and thanksgiving through the mercy of a loving God. The offering was accepted, the prayer answered.

another. This was supposed to be done to the glory of God—would He be embarrassed? Would we? Not many of us were optimistic.

Easter morning was gray and the air smelled more like winter than spring. As the organ played the prelude, we filed into our places in the choir loft. The pastor offered his morning prayer. We raised our books in unison and opened them, focusing on the director as she raised her arms. Then we sang. Parts that had never been quite

Not just at Easter, but also all through the year, whenever we sing a new song for the Lord, whenever we proclaim His salvation and give Him praise, He takes our imperfections and failures and produces beauty. As He has been, He continues to be: a God of resurrection.

Pamela Kennedy is a freelance writer of short stories, articles, essays, and children's books, as well as the mother of three children. She currently resides in Honolulu, Hawaii.

THE TRIUMPHAL ENTRY INTO JERUSALEM

Mark 11:1–10

And when they came nigh to Jerusalem, unto Bethphage and Bethany, at the mount of Olives, he sendeth forth two of his disciples,

And saith unto them, Go your way into the village over against you: and as soon as ye be entered into it, ye shall find a colt tied, whereon never man sat; loose him, and bring him.

And if any man say unto you, Why do ye this? say ye that the Lord hath need of him; and straightway he will send him hither.

And they went their way, and found the colt tied by the door without in a place where two ways met; and they loose him.

And certain of them that stood there said unto them, What do ye, loosing the colt?

And they said unto them even as Jesus had commanded: and they let them go.

And they brought the colt to Jesus, and cast their garments on him; and he sat upon him.

And many spread their garments in the way: and others cut down branches off the trees, and strawed them in the way.

And they that went before, and they that followed, cried, saying, Hosanna; Blessed is he that cometh in the name of the Lord:

Blessed be the kingdom of our father David, that cometh in the name of the Lord: Hosanna in the highest.

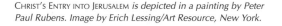

CHRIST'S ENTRY INTO JERUSALEM *is depicted in a painting by Peter Paul Rubens. Image by Erich Lessing/Art Resource, New York.*

THE LAST SUPPER

Luke 22:14–23

And when the hour was come, he sat down, and the twelve apostles with him.

And he said unto them, With desire I have desired to eat this passover with you before I suffer:

For I say unto you, I will not any more eat thereof, until it be fulfilled in the kingdom of God.

And he took the cup, and gave thanks, and said, Take this, and divide it among yourselves:

For I say unto you, I will not drink of the fruit of the vine, until the kingdom of God shall come.

And he took bread, and gave thanks, and brake it, and gave unto them, saying, This is my body which is given for you: this do in remembrance of me.

Likewise also the cup after supper, saying, This cup is the new testament in my blood, which is shed for you.

But, behold, the hand of him that betrayeth me is with me on the table.

And truly the Son of man goeth, as it was determined: but woe unto that man by whom he is betrayed!

And they began to inquire among themselves, which of them it was that should do this thing.

THE LAST SUPPER *is portrayed in a painting by Peter Paul Rubens. Image by Erich Lessing/Art Resource, New York.*

The Washing of the Disciples' Feet

John 13:4–9,12–17

He riseth from supper, and laid aside his garments; and took a towel, and girded himself.

After that he poureth water into a basin, and began to wash the disciples' feet, and to wipe them with the towel wherewith he was girded.

Then cometh he to Simon Peter: and Peter saith unto him, Lord, dost thou wash my feet?

Jesus answered and said unto him, What I do thou knowest not now; but thou shalt know hereafter.

Peter saith unto him, Thou shalt never wash my feet. Jesus answered him, If I wash thee not, thou hast no part with me.

Simon Peter saith unto him, Lord, not my feet only, but also my hands and my head.

So after he had washed their feet, and had taken his garments, and was set down again, he said unto them, Know ye what I have done to you?

Ye call me Master and Lord: and ye say well; for so I am.

If I then, your Lord and Master, have washed your feet; ye also ought to wash one another's feet.

For I have given you an example, that ye should do as I have done to you.

Verily, verily, I say unto you, The servant is not greater than his lord; neither he that is sent greater than he that sent him.

If ye know these things, happy are ye if ye do them.

The lesson of Christ Washing the Apostles' Feet is shown in a painting by Peter Paul Rubens. Image by Erich Lessing/Art Resource, New York.

THE CRUCIFIXION

John 19:17–18, 23–30

And he bearing his cross went forth into a place called the place of a skull, which is called in the Hebrew Golgotha:

Where they crucified him, and two other with him, on either side one, and Jesus in the midst.

Then the soldiers, when they had crucified Jesus, took his garments, and made four parts, to every soldier a part; and also his coat: now the coat was without seam, woven from the top throughout.

They said therefore among themselves, Let us not rend it, but cast lots for it, whose it shall be: that the scripture might be fulfilled, which saith, They parted my raiment among them, and for my vesture they did cast lots. These things therefore the soldiers did.

Now there stood by the cross of Jesus his mother, and his mother's sister, Mary the wife of Cleophas, and Mary Magdalene.

When Jesus therefore saw his mother, and the disciple standing by, whom he loved, he saith unto his mother, Woman, behold thy son!

Then saith he to the disciple, Behold thy mother! And from that hour that disciple took her unto his own home.

After this, Jesus knowing that all things were now accomplished, that the scripture might be fulfilled, saith, I thirst.

Now there was set a vessel full of vinegar: and they filled a sponge with vinegar, and put it upon hyssop, and put it to his mouth.

When Jesus therefore had received the vinegar, he said, It is finished: and he bowed his head, and gave up the ghost.

The agony of THE ELEVATION OF THE CROSS *is captured in a painting by Peter Paul Rubens. Image by Arnaudet/Réunion des Musées Nationaux/Art Resource, New York.*

Jesus' Appearance to the Disciples

John 20:19–29

Then the same day at evening, being the first day of the week, when the doors were shut where the disciples were assembled for fear of the Jews, came Jesus and stood in the midst, and saith unto them, Peace be unto you. And when he had so said, he showed unto them his hands and his side. Then were the disciples glad, when they saw the Lord.

Then said Jesus to them again, Peace be unto you: as my Father hath sent me, even so send I you.

And when he had said this, he breathed on them, and saith unto them, Receive ye the Holy Ghost:

Whosesoever sins ye remit, they are remitted unto them; and whosesoever sins ye retain, they are retained.

But Thomas, one of the twelve, called Didymus, was not with them when Jesus came.

The other disciples therefore said unto him, We have seen the Lord. But he said unto them, Except I shall see in his hands the print of the nails, and put my finger into the print of the nails, and thrust my hand into his side, I will not believe.

And after eight days again his disciples were within, and Thomas with them: then came Jesus, the doors being shut, and stood in the midst, and said, Peace be unto you.

Then saith he to Thomas, Reach hither thy finger, and behold my hands; and reach hither thy hand, and thrust it into my side: and be not faithless, but believing.

And Thomas answered and said unto him, My Lord and my God.

Jesus saith unto him, Thomas, because thou hast seen me, thou hast believed: blessed are they that have not seen, and yet have believed.

THE INCREDULITY OF THOMAS *is expressed in a painting by Peter Paul Rubens. Image by Museo Reale di Belle Arti, Antwerp/Art Resource, New York.*

The White Mountains wear the early colors of spring in this panoramic view of Mount Kineo and Carr Mountain in White Mountains National Park, New Hampshire. Photograph by William H. Johnson.

When I Survey the Wondrous Cross

Isaac Watts

When I survey the wondrous Cross
Where the young Prince of Glory died,
My richest gain I count but loss,
And pour contempt on all my pride.

Forbid it, Lord, that I should boast,
Save in the Cross of Christ, my God:
All the vain things that charm me most,
I sacrifice them to His blood.

See, from His head, His hands, His feet,
Sorrow and love flow mingled down!
Did e'er such love and sorrow meet,
Or thorns compose so rich a crown?

Were the whole realm of nature mine,
That were an offering far too small;
Love so amazing, so divine,
Demands my soul, my life, my all.

Good Morning! Christ Is Risen

Raphael Harwood Miller

Without Christ's Resurrection, life is a dream without substance,
a progress without purpose, and a journey without destination.
 Every fresh adventure of the human spirit;
   every new crusade against embattled wrong;
   every daring excursion across the frontiers of knowledge;
   every costly devotion to freedom's cause;
   every undaunted endeavor for a world of peace and good will;
   every tireless struggle for justice and equality;
   every heroic martyrdom for faith—all, all go forth
     under the cloudless Resurrection morning
     whose sun shall stand still
     and whose light shall not fail until the work is done.

THROUGH MY WINDOW

Pamela Kennedy

PILATE'S WIFE

Claudia's sleep was disturbed. Her husband had left before sunrise, called to the Fortress of Antonia to adjudicate in a capital case brought against Jesus of Nazareth. Now she tossed in her luxurious bed. Spring breezes rustled the palms in the garden below while cooing doves and the soft splash of fountains created a haunting rhythm. A figure in white, surrounded by men and women, appeared in her dreams. The figure turned and Claudia glimpsed a familiar face. He was a teacher and healer, they said, a miracle worker sent from God.

Ever since arriving in Jerusalem from their palace in Caesarea Philippi, Claudia had been drawn to this enigmatic man. Wearing a disguise, she had often slipped from the palace to listen as He spoke of a loving God. The God Jesus described was unlike any of the Roman gods Claudia worshiped; yet His words rang true in her heart. He tenderly healed the blind and deaf and some said He had even raised a man from the dead. Just a handful of days ago Jesus had angered religious leaders by entering Jerusalem to shouts of "Hosanna" and the praises of the people. Then, shortly after that, He strode through the temple courtyard, overturning tables, scattering livestock, lashing out at the moneychangers with a whip made of knotted cords. Before all the assembled pilgrims and priests, He loudly condemned those engaged in commerce as defilers of God's house. Tempers flared and the embarrassed Jewish leaders gathered to plot their revenge.

Now the cacophony of bleating livestock, wailing women, and shouting men swirled in her dream like a gathering storm. The image of Jesus grew more distinct. Tears streamed from His eyes

---

Wearing a disguise, she had often slipped from the palace to listen as He spoke of a loving God.

---

as He reached His arms towards her. She saw His hands, pierced and bleeding. Then He spoke, "Father, forgive them." A cold fear gripped Claudia. She was suffocating, drowning in a sea of terror. A scream woke her and she realized it was her own. For a moment she lay there, trembling in the sweat-damp sheets. Then, recalling her nightmare, she leaped up and called for her servant.

The girl ran to her mistress's bedchamber, her eyes wide, "Yes, my lady?"

"Come here," Claudia commanded. Grabbing a sheet of parchment she quickly wrote her message: *Don't have anything to do with that innocent man, for I have suffered a great deal today in a dream because of Him.*

She hastily folded the sheet, sealing it with a circle of hot, red wax. "Take this quickly to your master. He is sitting in judgment at the Fortress of Antonia, hearing a case against Jesus the Nazarene. Hurry! This is a matter of life and death!"

The servant dashed from her mistress's chamber. The minutes dragged into one hour, then another, and Claudia's fear grew. Finally, she grabbed a plain dark cloak and wrapped a linen shawl over her head. She left the palace quietly, heading for the judgment hall. Perhaps she could do something before it was too late.

Pilgrims jostled her as she wove through the thronging crowd. Suddenly, she was completely stopped as a wall of people pressed back from the street, opening a path for someone. Claudia pushed her shoulder between two large men, gaining a view of the strange procession. Roman soldiers, swords drawn, walked before a man bearing a huge wooden crossbeam. His back and face were swollen from a beating and He wore a rudely crafted crown of thorns. Pilate's wife leaned in, trying to catch a glimpse of the man's face. Then suddenly He stumbled, dropping the beam to the paving stones. One of the soldiers strode into the crowd, grabbed a pilgrim by his cloak, and then ordered him to pick up the beam and carry it for the condemned man. As he did so, the man with the crown straightened up, turned, and stared into Claudia's eyes. The look was one of sorrow and love. She gasped. It was Jesus of Nazareth! She had failed and Pilate had condemned Him to death.

Quickly she hid her face from Him, spun around, and pushed her way through the angry mob. She ran blindly back to the safety of Herod's palace, ducking through the marble porticoes, dashing up the steps to her private quarters. She was sobbing by the time she reached her room. She had tried to warn her husband, tried to stop the fulfillment of her nightmare, but it was all in vain. Convinced more than ever that she was somehow to blame for the condemnation of this righteous man, Claudia's heart ached with guilt. How would she live with this burden? Then, quietly, almost like a shadow, the image from her dream returned. She saw the figure of Jesus once more, the outstretched arms, the tears, the pierced hands. Then she heard the words again: "Father, forgive them." Claudia bowed her head into her trembling hands and whispered through her tears: "Oh, Father, forgive me, too." As her sobs stilled, she seemed to hear a voice in the rustling of the palms below whisper, "My daughter, I already have."

_____

Original artwork by Meredith Johnson.

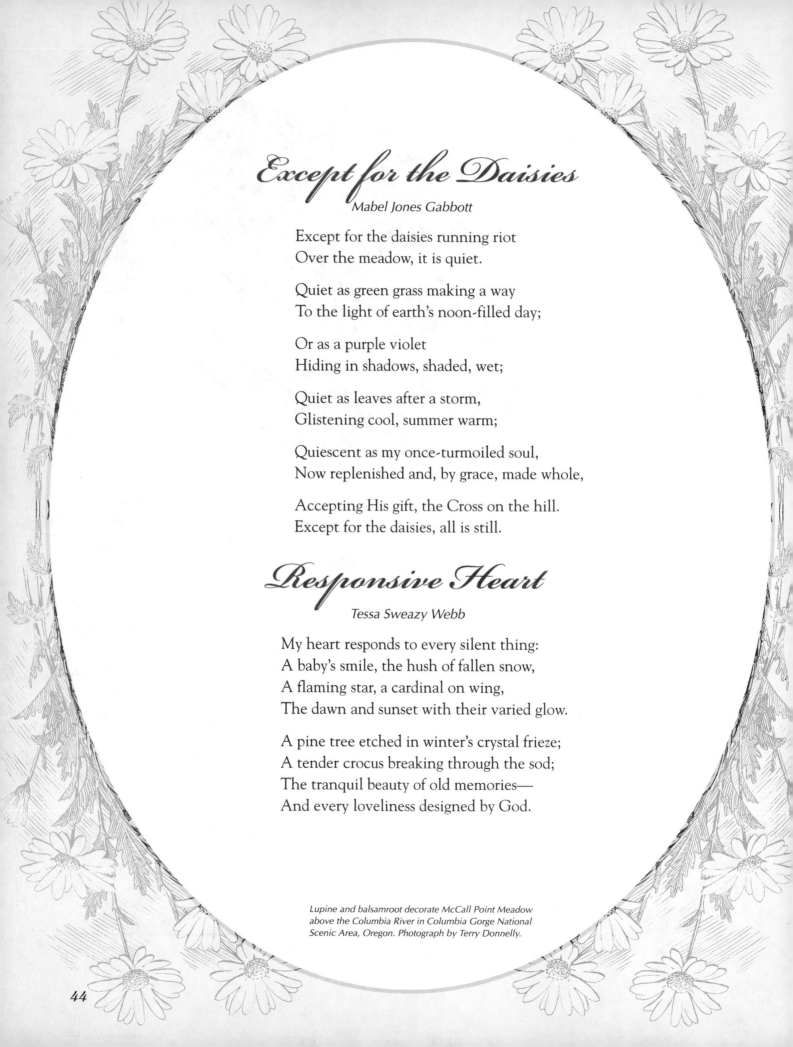

Except for the Daisies

Mabel Jones Gabbott

Except for the daisies running riot
Over the meadow, it is quiet.

Quiet as green grass making a way
To the light of earth's noon-filled day;

Or as a purple violet
Hiding in shadows, shaded, wet;

Quiet as leaves after a storm,
Glistening cool, summer warm;

Quiescent as my once-turmoiled soul,
Now replenished and, by grace, made whole,

Accepting His gift, the Cross on the hill.
Except for the daisies, all is still.

Responsive Heart

Tessa Sweazy Webb

My heart responds to every silent thing:
A baby's smile, the hush of fallen snow,
A flaming star, a cardinal on wing,
The dawn and sunset with their varied glow.

A pine tree etched in winter's crystal frieze;
A tender crocus breaking through the sod;
The tranquil beauty of old memories—
And every loveliness designed by God.

*Lupine and balsamroot decorate McCall Point Meadow
above the Columbia River in Columbia Gorge National
Scenic Area, Oregon. Photograph by Terry Donnelly.*

The Easter Message

Margaret Rorke

Of all the words that have been said
Throughout recorded time
The angel's news: "He is not dead!"
Is, doubtless, most sublime.
It underscores Christ's work and worth;
It proves His promise true
And offers hope to all on earth
Like nothing else can do.

Apostles bowed by loss and grief,
By shaken faith and fear,
Sought evidence before belief
Like many now and here.
He gave them proof—the proof we heed
On every Easter Day—
The proof Christ lives and is, indeed,
The Truth, the Life, the Way.

Song of Spring

Jane Hillsman

The pansy's splash of color
    seems a ruse to draw the eye
    away from tulips, tall and stiff,
    in pink rows marching by.

The yellow jasmine's fragrance
    and the violet's perfume
    like the scent of heady incense
    permeates my little room.

But the flame of all the redbuds
    reaching upward to the sky
    fills my racing heart with music
    like a great choir passing by.

And I catch my breath in wonder
    as I hear the redbuds sing,
    arrayed in all their glory,
    "Oh, hosanna to our King."

Luola's Chapel, built by James Sprunt in 1915 for his wife, Luola Murchison, stands at the entrance to Orton Plantation Gardens, on the Cape Fear River, near Wilmington, North Carolina. Photograph by Ken DeQuaine.

FROM MY GARDEN JOURNAL

Lisa Ragan

DELPHINIUMS

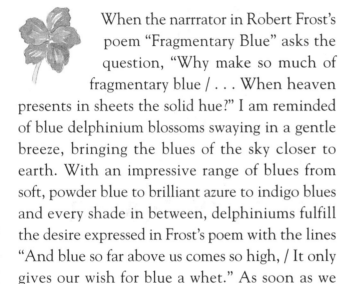

When the narrrator in Robert Frost's poem "Fragmentary Blue" asks the question, "Why make so much of fragmentary blue / . . . When heaven presents in sheets the solid hue?" I am reminded of blue delphinium blossoms swaying in a gentle breeze, bringing the blues of the sky closer to earth. With an impressive range of blues from soft, powder blue to brilliant azure to indigo blues and every shade in between, delphiniums fulfill the desire expressed in Frost's poem with the lines "And blue so far above us comes so high, / It only gives our wish for blue a whet." As soon as we have one of those sunny spring days with an impossibly blue sky that seems to lift everyone's spirits, I start thinking about delphiniums.

Delphiniums were named by the people of ancient Greece, who likened the look of the unopened bud to that of a dolphin. Sometimes the delphinium bears the common name *larkspur*, but the true larkspur is actually an annual of the genus *Consolida* whereas the delphinium is a perennial of the genus *Delphinium*. Both flowers are members of the buttercup family, *Ranunculaceae*.

Climate Considerations

Luckily, delphiniums can add exquisite color to almost any garden region. As a result of development over the last hundred years, gardeners today can choose from more than two hundred different species within the *Delphinium* genus. Nearly every garden can be home to delphiniums, with their range of heights, colors, and temperaments. Whether one gardens in a dry, sandy, desert-like environment or in a wet woodland, a delphinium hybrid can be found to thrive there and in nearly every climate in between.

Blues and Other Color Choices

Like their original namesake leaping through the waves, the larger hybrids produce tall, graceful spires that can reach seven or eight feet; whereas some of the more delicate dwarf varieties,

DELPHINIUM

such as the Magic Fountains cultivars, reach twenty-eight inches at full height. Color options not only include every imaginable tint of blue but also shades of purple, lavender, mauve, salmon, pink, red, white, and yellow, as well as bicolor varieties. One interesting characteristic of this extraordinary plant is that the delphinium reigns as one of the few perennials that can offer flower hues in all three primary colors. How can any gardener, whether new or experienced, not adore a plant that has those color choices?

If your color favorites are purple, mauve, and white, as well as the range of blues, Belladonna delphiniums comprise dwarf varieties that grow to three and a half feet high and can feature blossoms in these choices. For those gardeners who choose to flaunt the delphinium's primary color palette, red can be found in *D. cardinale* and yellow in *D. semibarbatum*. For those of us who seek the famous blues, a number of blue options work well in the primary colors, and *D. grandiflorum* Blue Mirror has proven a popular choice. Other spectacular blues in the *D. elatum* hybrid group are Blue Nile, Loch Leven, and Blue Dawn. Lord Butler, also a *D. elatum*, is pale blue with lilac touches. Mighty Atom is a vivid violet and Bruce is a deep purple, for those who enjoy richness and depth of color in the garden. From the soft white of Sandpiper to the bright yellow of Sungleam, delphiniums offer the gardener a treasure of color choices.

Spring Planting

Small plants or rooted cuttings can be planted in early spring in an open site in full sun. Nearby trees, hedges, fences, and buildings can force the plants to grow too tall and leggy as they seek light. Whereas a windbreak can be helpful in protecting these delicate flowers from blustery gales, a windbreak planted too close will result in gangly plants. Delphiniums must be staked, since a typical rainstorm can devastate this delicate flower. A cage of dried bamboo provides the ideal stake by providing needed support without excessively restricting the plants.

The soil of the planting site also must be considered carefully. It must be nutrient-rich, another reason to avoid hedges and trees, which can rob hungry delphiniums of their needed nutrition. If you want to try growing delphiniums in containers, be sure to keep them well watered and fertilized throughout the early spring and summer.

A Second Blooming Season

The typical blooming time of a mere three weeks leaves most delphinium lovers hungry for more, and this can be achieved with careful attention to the plants after flowering. Remove the flower stalks, allowing the foliage to remain. Once the yellowing leaves begin to brown, cut the plant down to ground level. This encourages new shoots and a rewarding second blooming season.

Even with the somewhat lengthy list of growing requirements, we gardeners who thrill at the sight of blue blossoms proclaim the delphinium to be well worth the effort. A glimpse of "fragmentary blue" can be all it takes to inspire the care and attention necessary to reap a garden full of beautiful delphiniums reaching for the sky.

Lisa Ragan tends her small but mighty urban garden in Nashville, Tennessee, with the help of her son, Trenton, and her two Shih Tzus, Curry and Cayenne.

April Winds

Sudie Stuart Hager

These are the steeds, whose wildly galloping hoofs
We heard in winter lanes. They plagued our dreams
By thundering in hordes across our roofs
With savage neighs crescendoing into screams.

Their wild, swift feet at last are tamed and shod;
Their fierce throats docile, uttering no sound;
Their daring natures reconciled to plod
Where spring is strewing gold along the ground.

The steeds that charged down from the winter hills
Tread gently now through April's daffodils.

Daffodil's Return

Bliss Carman

What matter if the sun be lost?
What matter though the sky be gray?
There's joy enough about the house,
For Daffodil comes home today.

There's news of swallows on the air,
There's word of April on the way,
They're calling flowers within the street,
And Daffodil comes home today.

Oh, who would care what fate may bring,
Or what the years may take away!
There's life enough within the hour,
For Daffodil comes home today.

Two horses enjoy a warm spring day surrounded by the lovely flowers of West Shores Acres Display Garden in Oregon. Photograph by Dick Dietrich.

LEGENDARY AMERICANS

Laurie Hunter

JAMES WHITCOMB RILEY

James Whitcomb Riley has been called the "People's Poet" and the "Robert Burns of America." His characters and plain witticisms have become standards in American culture. In his writing Riley celebrates the simplicity of rural life and the forthright nature of the common people. He evinces an honest appreciation for the difficult lives of ordinary folks and respects the sincerity and steadfast courage of the average man, woman, and child.

Little Orphant Annie's come to our house to stay / An' wash the cups an' saucers up, an' brush the crumbs away.

"Little Orphant Annie"

Also nicknamed the "Hoosier Poet" because of his use of the phonetic spelling and accents of Middle America, Riley personally charmed audiences at public readings. He spent many years traveling the United States with other well-known writers, such as Mark Twain, for public performances. During the 1880s, Riley had engagements almost every night in which he alternated poetry and prose stories with character sketches. Henry Wadsworth Longfellow, already a respected poet, encouraged him early in his career and publicly described him as a "true poet."

Riley was born in Greenfield, Indiana, in 1849, the third of six children. The importance of family is evident in his personal writings and in the fact that he dedicated many of his works to his siblings. His father, Reuben Riley, was a lawyer, as well as a locally renowned speaker, and had been an officer in the Union Army during the Civil War. Riley's mother, Elizabeth Marine Riley, published poetry in local papers and enjoyed writing short plays for neighborhood children's productions. Riley always held her in high esteem and it is from her that Riley inherited his enthusiasm for performing.

Riley, advised against pursuing poetry by his father, left home at an early age to make his own way. He worked as a clerk in a shoe store and then tried, unsuccessfully, selling Bibles. He had a fascinatingly brief career as a frontman for two traveling medicine shows during which he played the guitar, sang, performed comic skits, and basically honed his skills as an entertainer. Riley later referred to the members of the second show as "good straight boys, jolly chirping vagabonds like myself."

Riley was employed at local newspapers in the late 1870s and began to make serious efforts to publish his own material. Using different pseudonyms, he was able to develop his writing skills during that time. Throughout the 1870s and 1880s, Riley completed a remarkable body of work and, fortunately for the public, Indianapolis

James Whitcomb Riley. Photograph courtesy of the James Whitcomb Riley Memorial Association.

had become an important center of publishing.

In 1883, his first book of poetry, entitled *The Old Swimmin'-Hole and 'Leven More Poems*, was published by Riley and a partner. The one thousand copies printed were sold out in three

An' all us other childern, when the supper-things is done, / We set around the kitchen fire an' has the mostest fun.
"Little Orphant Annie"

months. In October 1883, a new publisher, Merrill Meigs & Company, re-published his book, its first literary release. Between the 1880s and 1920s, more than sixty books by Riley were published by this same company.

In addition to Mark Twain, Riley was significantly influenced by and also became good friends with Joel Chandler Harris, whose Uncle Remus stories already had introduced the

American public to the use of dialect in poetry.

Riley's most popular poem, "Little Orphant Annie," was first printed on November 15, 1885. The character of Annie was based on the personality of Mary Alice "Allie" Smith, an orphan who had moved into the Riley household in 1862 as a housekeeper in exchange for room and board. Originally the character's name was "Allie," but a typesetting error changed it to "Annie." Riley never corrected it because the poem was immediately popular with readers. The former housekeeper did not know she was the model for the beloved heroine until, in her seventies, she returned to Greenfield for a visit.

Riley believed that poems like "The Raggedy Man," "When the Frost Is on the Punkin'," and "The Days Gone By," in addition to "Little Orphant Annie," fulfilled the public's desire to read and hear "simple sentiments from the heart."

Riley died on July 22, 1916, from complications of a stroke. More than thirty-five thousand people attended his memorial services at the Indiana state capital.

Riley wrote over one thousand poems, all tributes to the expansive heart and values of the heartland.

NAME: James Whitcomb Riley

BORN: October 7, 1849, Greenfield, Indiana

ACCOMPLISHMENTS: One of the most popular poets of the nineteenth century.

DIED: July 22, 1916

QUOTE: "The most essential factor is persistence—the determination never to allow your energy or enthusiasm to be dampened by the discouragement that must inevitably come."

TRAVELER'S DIARY

D. Fran Morley

HOMES OF JAMES WHITCOMB RILEY
GREENFIELD AND INDIANAPOLIS, INDIANA

As a child growing up in Indiana, I was familiar with the works of Hoosier poet James Whitcomb Riley. I memorized "Little Orphant Annie" for a school production and then discovered that my father had once had the same assignment in elementary school. My father remained a fan of Riley his whole life and often recited bits of his poetry.

So, on a recent visit, I was happy to learn that Riley is still remembered fondly in my home state. In fact, his life is celebrated at two historic sites. At his birthplace, the "Old Home" in Greenfield, it is easy to see how his childhood was a major influence on his writing. In contrast, the home in Indianapolis, where he lived for the last twenty-three years of his life, demonstrates how his great success shaped his later years.

The Riley Museum Home on Lockerbie Street in Indianapolis is an impressive brick residence in a neighborhood of meticulously restored Victorian homes. I quickly learned that the Riley Home is a rarity because it is preserved, not restored. Riley's friends and fellow writers purchased it soon after

James Whitcomb Riley's childhood home. Photograph courtesy of Greenfield Parks and Recreation.

his death in 1916, and everything in it—from the carpets on the floors to the books on the shelves—is just as it was when Riley was alive.

Riley was very successful in his long career, so I was surprised to discover that he was not the owner of the six-bedroom home. A guide explained that, because Riley traveled a lot, he chose to live as a paying guest of dear friends. Riley lived like family, however; he participated in family decisions and often purchased items for the house, including the beautiful crystal gaslight chandelier in the dining room and the player piano in the parlor.

The home, I learned, was one of the first in the city with both central heat and indoor plumbing. It was fascinating to see how rainwater was hand-pumped to a tank in the attic to flow down to the bath and to sinks in each of the bedrooms.

Riley's desk and many personal items are in his second-floor bedroom, but the portrait of his beloved dog, Lockerbie, is a tender sight. According to the guide, the small poodle had the run of the house and could frequently be found under the dining room table.

I could have spent more time looking at the beautiful house, but I wanted to explore Riley's roots, and for that I had to go to his birthplace.

I made the short drive to Greenfield, to see the three-bedroom frame house that had been home to attorney Reuben Riley and his family. The Rileys lived a prosperous, small-town life in this house until Reuben Riley was wounded during the Civil War. Hard times then forced the family to move to a smaller house, but young James vowed to buy back the big house for his mother some day. She passed away before he could do so, but, in 1893, he finally purchased the home and allowed other family members to move in.

Riley Museum Home. Photograph courtesy of the James Whitcomb Riley Memorial Association.

Few items in this house are original, but it is furnished as it would have been in Riley's boyhood. The Riley family Bible is in a glass case in the parlor next to a rocking chair that Reuben Riley made for his wife, Elizabeth. An Old Home hostess explained that Riley's mother rocked her babies in that chair and drew her last breath in it. There are many family photos in the house, including one of Mary Alice Smith, the young housekeeper whom Riley later immortalized as Little Orphant Annie.

As I walked around the house, I discovered that the house itself is perhaps the most significant artifact because of the way Riley used it in his writing. The cubbyhole in the children's bedroom and the upstairs rafter room are just as Riley described them. The hostess brought the house to life by reciting the appropriate poem for each room, complete with theatrics and old-fashioned Hoosier dialect.

Items from Riley's long career are in the museum next door to the Old Home. I was surprised to find out that, just as a celebrity would do today, Riley used his fame to endorse products. One display included Riley canned fruit, Riley cigars, and even Riley salt and seasonings. Other memorabilia include a handwritten poem on the death of President Ulysses S. Grant, an invitation to join President Theodore Roosevelt for a White House dinner, and many of Riley's personal items, such as his top hat and cane.

A unique photo collage on display shows many of Riley's contemporaries, including Bret Harte, Booth Tarkington, Walt Whitman, and Mark Twain. It amused me to find out that Twain and Riley were friendly rivals. Twain was often miffed if Riley received top billing when they shared a stage.

Before I left Greenfield, I stopped to see the statue of Riley that thousands of schoolchildren built with penny donations a few years after his death. I was told that schoolchildren still come to the statue every October, during the James Whitcomb Riley Festival, to lay flowers at the feet of Indiana's best-loved poet. My father would have liked that.

When not gallivanting around the country, travel writer Fran Morley spends time with her husband and their cat, Gracie, in beautiful Fairhope, Alabama.

A Feather
Josephine Millard

A meadowlark sings, far above
The quiet and empty field,
A song prophetic of the good
The coming months will yield.

A tiny shaft of tinted light
Comes drifting down to trace,
As gently as a breath subdued,
Its shadow on my face.

A feather from a singing lark,
A symbol of the spring,
Rests gently on my startled cheek,
One moment there to cling.

As fragile as a fleeting dream,
It lifts and flutters on.
My hand, too slow to grasp and hold,
Moves after it is gone.

A common yellow-shafted flicker has left a feather on an evening primrose in Mackinaw State Forest, Michigan. Photograph by Darryl R. Beers.

Spring Faith

R. H. Grenville

So swiftly sunlight pierces cloud,
So surely day from night is born,
So faithfully returns the flower,
I wonder that the heart should mourn.

For beauty hidden from our sight
A little while returns again.
No lovely thing is ever lost;
No prayer is ever prayed in vain.

Each springtime sees the snows depart,
The leafless bough renew its bloom,
And, comfort for the whole world's heart,
Christ emerging from the tomb.

*The cherished lily of the valley each spring rewards
those who appreciate its delicate flowers. Photograph
by Spectrum/H. Armstrong Roberts.*

THE ROBIN'S SONG

Eben E. Rexford

Last night I heard
    a robin singing in the rain;
And the raindrops' patter
    made a sweet refrain,
Making all the sweeter
    the music of the strain.

So, I thought, when trouble comes,
    as trouble will,
Why should I stop singing?
    Just beyond the hill
It may be that sunshine
    floods the green world still.

He who faces trouble
    with a heart of cheer
Makes the burden lighter.
    If there falls a tear,
Sweeter is the cadence
    in the song we hear.

I have learned your lesson,
    bird of dappled wing,
Listening to your music
    with its promises of spring:
When the storm cloud darkens,
    then is the time to sing.

Rhododendron provide lovely mounds of pale blossoms along a woodland path. Photograph by LeFever/Grushow from Grant Heilman.

BITS & PIECES

Wake from thy nest, robin redbreast!
Sing, birds, in every furrow,
And from each bill let music shrill
Give my fair Love good morrow!

—*Thomas Heywood*

Spring. Of all seasons most gratuitous,
Is fold of untaught flower, is race of water,
Is earth's most multiple, excited daughter.

—*Philip Larkin*

Measure your health by your sympathy with morning and spring. If there is no response in you to the awakening of nature—if the prospect of an early morning walk does not banish sleep, if the warble of the first bluebird does not thrill you—know that the morning and spring of your life are past. Thus may you feel your pulse.

—*Henry David Thoreau*

60

When in our music God is glorified,
And adoration leaves no room for pride,
It is as though the whole creation cried "Alleluia!"
—*Frederick Pratt Green*

In spring more mortal singers than belong
To any one place cover us with song.
Thrush, bluebird, blackbird, sparrow, and robin throng.
—*Robert Frost*

Birds delight
Day and Night.
—*William Blake*

Mockingbirds don't do one thing but make music for us to enjoy. They don't eat up people's gardens, don't nest in corncribs; they don't do one thing but sing their hearts out for us. That's why it's a sin to kill a mockingbird.
—*Harper Lee*

COLLECTOR'S CORNER

Laurie Hunter

PORCELAIN BIRD FIGURINES

Grandmother Louise just shakes her head. "I don't know how I have so many . . ." she says, as she looks at the bird figurines perched on nearly every surface of her home. "It just happened."

There are bird figurines tucked into teacups in the china cabinet. Others have "flown" to the top of the bookshelves. And still others sit perched on tables and in nooks. Nestled at the center of this crowded bird sanctuary sits my grandmother.

Every bird figurine Grandmother Louise owns came to her as a gift, and she loves each unique and unusual figurine—regardless of its monetary value. Because of its diversity, her collection offers endless joy to owner and visitors.

Grandmother has fine porcelain birds as well as vintage ones of varying value. For instance, among her favorites is a small glazed bird that was formed and fired by her brother-in-law then painted and glazed by her sister. I too have my favorites that I look for on each visit. My first glance is always to the graceful, silky gray and pink cranes in flight, one tucked under the other's wings, by Lladró of Spain. Then I look for the exquisite yet brilliant rose flamingoes wrapped around the tiny Limoges box. And I love the sweet pair of hummingbirds and brilliant male cardinal. Both of these beautiful Lenox porcelain figurines mirror their real-life cousins at the feeders on the other side of the dining room window.

Porcelain has been collectible since the thirteenth century, when Marco Polo returned from China and brought with him a porcelain vase. Subsequently, others returned from China—and later, Japan—with more examples of porcelain wares, increasing the awareness and demand in Europe for those objects.

Although China invented the process of making porcelain, England perfected the process of firing and glazing fine porcelain by the late 1700s. By the dawn of the Victorian Age, many manufacturers throughout England and Europe were producing magnificent porcelain figurines, many of which are prized today. Factories of Europe such as Dresden and Meissen in Germany, Royal Worcester in England, and Limoges in France have all produced a line of porcelain collectible birds. Many of these antique porcelain birds are valued highly in the world of antique collectibles.

Few, if any, of Grandmother Louise's birds would be considered rare or valuable by art appraisers; but these gifts, which have come to her from many friends throughout the years of her life, are highly valued by Grandmother. These porcelain birds sit on the shelves and on the tables of her home as tangible reminders of love and of that which Grandmother most cherishes—nature, family, and friendship.

Birds of a Feather

As you begin to collect bird figurines or add to an existing collection, the following information may be helpful.

Historical Development

• Porcelain was first made in China in about the seventh century, A.D.

• Europeans tried for several centuries to discover the exact method by which porcelain was made in China and Japan. They came close with soft-paste porcelain, but did not solve the mystery of the process for making the preferred hard-paste porcelain until the early 1700s.

Porcelain Defined

• Porcelain is a type of ceramic that is hard, fine-grained, white, translucent, and consists of the biscuit (a pure clay that has been fired) and the glaze.

• Hard-paste, or true, porcelain was first made in China in a primitive form in the seventh century, A.D. This true porcelain is made from stone ground to powder and mixed with a white clay called kaolin.

• Soft-paste porcelain, a mixture of clay and ground glass, is more brittle than hard-paste porcelain.

• Josiah Spode added bone ash to the materials used for hard-paste porcelain, which made the porcelain resistant to chipping. Spode developed this type of porcelain, known as bone china, around 1800.

Suggestions for Getting Started

• Begin your hunt at estate sales, antique shops, thrift shops, and flea markets.

• Narrow your collection by choosing birds of a favorite species or a certain manufacturer or time period.

• Select pieces that have been signed by the artist or those bearing the mark of a recognized manufacturer.

Dogwood at Spring *is a limited edition bisque porcelain and bronze sculpture by artist Pierrre Lefebvre. Image courtesy of Lenox.*

Manufacturers of Bird Figurines

• Messein, in Germany, was the first company to successfully produce hard-paste porcelain in Europe. The company opened its doors in 1710 and continues to craft fine figurines, including birds, today.

• Royal Worcester, established in 1751, produced bird figurines painted by British and American artists from 1935 to 1962.

• Sevres and Limoges, in France, have rich traditions of highly decorative wares.

• Lladró, a Spanish manufacturer, has made a number of exquisite bird figurines since its founding in 1953.

• Lefton, in Illinois, made bird figurines from about 1946 to 1964.

• U.S. manufacturers Lenox and Boehm Porcelain each have a line of bird figurines.

Laurie Hunter lives in Leiper's Fork, Tennessee, with her husband and two children.

A Sweet Young Girl

Edna Staples

Springtime is a sweet young girl
    with flowers in her hair;
Apple blossoms, daffodils,
    and soft perfumes are everywhere.
Tripping lightly as she comes,
    dancing with the breeze,
She waves her wand with magic rare
    and clothes the stark, bare trees.

She laughs and plays with little things,
    like pups and baby sheep;
And when they're tired, she sprinkles them
    with sunshine as they sleep.

A change of mood, now clouds and tears,
    and a pouting, puckered face—
The storm will end and she will again
    have all her tears erased.

She brings us hope and happiness,
    and also a special thrill
To know that we can start again,
    and that, like her, we will.
Springtime is a sweet young girl
    with flowers in her hair;
And as she dances o'er the hills,
    sweet perfumes float through the air.

Spring Has Just Begun

Leah K. Nutter

She sings as she sheds her winter-white gown
    And weaves white blossoms for a crown.
She paints with colors so rich and so new,
    And pearls many petals with a light morning dew.
She stirs the earth and all awake;
    Tender new life is here.
She clothes the ground with a soft green cape
    And sprinkles violets everywhere.
She bathes young and old with a shower of rain
    And nurtures each one in the warmth of the sun.
All nature stands poised to help start her reign,
    For Mother Spring's touch has just now begun.

The yellow flower clusters of golden chain trees highlight the velvet purple of flowering alliums in the VanDusen Botanical Garden in Vancouver, British Columbia. Photograph by Dennis Frates.

SLICE OF LIFE
Edna Jaques

DREAMIN'

I have a world in which to roam,
  A tree a thousand miles from home
That I have never even seen—
  And yet I know its branches green
Will give me shade some happy day
  Beside a lake long miles away.

There is a beach of pure white sand,
  An island in a far-off strand,
Where I shall walk with happy feet,
  Where tall palms overhead will meet,
Where green and scarlet birds will fly
  Beneath a golden tropic sky.

There is a spring, whose waters flow
  along a creek bed cold as snow,
That I shall drink with eagerness
  Flavored with mint and watercress,
To quench a thirst that I have known
  Within my very flesh and bone.

There is a house beneath whose beams
  I shall catch up with faith and dreams,
Before a fire warm and bright;
  Outside the walls the lonely Night
Will beat upon the doorways stout,
  But love has come to keep him out.

Someone foretold this kindly fate,
And so I bide my time and wait.

A young woman pauses to daydream in an original painting,
THE EGG BASKET, *by Robert Duncan. Copyright © Robert Duncan.*
All rights reserved. Image provided by Robert Duncan Studios.

HANDMADE HEIRLOOM

Melissa Lester

WIND CHIMES

After long months burrowed indoors, I welcome springtime beckoning me to venture outside again. All around, the sounds of spring whisper their invitation to witness nature's splendid rebirth. In "An Ode Upon a Question Moved," seventeenth-century poet Lord Herbert of Cherbury penned,

> The well accorded Birds did sing
> Their hymns unto the pleasant time,
> And in a sweet consorted chime
> Did welcome in the chearful Spring.

For many gardeners, even before the birds return to announce the arrival of warmer weather, spring's call comes from wind chimes suspended in the garden. Today wind chimes are the most popular garden accessory in the country, estimated to have a place in eighty-five percent of American households. As decorative art, a source of pleasing random sounds, or a finely crafted musical instrument, wind chimes simultaneously relax and invigorate those who are nearby.

Many cultures have crafted wind ornaments, but the ancient Chinese developed the most elegant form. The Chinese began crafting metal wind bells around 1000 B.C. for musical accompaniments. The clapperless bells were hung in sets of graduated sizes and sounded with mallets. The elaborate designs of the cast or carved chimes featured dragons as a common theme. The Chinese attached wind chimes by the hundreds, even thousands, to the eaves of certain structures. When a breeze passed through, the resulting resonance and vibration of sound was almost overwhelming.

By the fourth century B.C., Japanese artisans had modified the Chinese wind bells by adding a piece called a *sail* or *clapper* to their bronze bells. Suspended inside a bell, the sail would catch a breeze and strike the chime. In the early days of Japanese wind chimes, the bells were communal property. But between the 1300s and 1500s, A.D.,

---

Many ordinary materials make attractive chimes.

---

wind chimes became available to individuals. These smaller, lighter wind bells were called *furin*. The enchanting sounds of wind chimes drew townspeople out to view the wares brought by furin peddlers. The hand-painted, bell-shaped glass designs were suspended from poles that the peddlers would carry on their backs. Furin is still the wind chime known to Japanese culture.

Appreciation for wind chimes has grown steadily throughout the centuries. The skilled artisans who craft chimes today bridge the gap between the ancient and contemporary worlds. A variety of materials, such as metal, bamboo, glass, and ceramics, may be used in the design of these chimes. With mathematical precision, artisans calculate for musical chimes how long each cylinder should be to achieve a certain note. Many factors determine the quality of the sound, including the type of material chosen and its length, temper, thickness, and diameter. In order to make the chimes a precise musical instrument, the artisan must be exacting in measurements and construction.

A less technically challenging wind chime can be made as a gift for a friend or family member that reflects an individual's hobby or a favorite collection. Any objects with visual appeal that would make a pleasant tinkling sound when struck together by a soft wind can be used. For example, a wind chime fashioned from antique silverware can add whimsical charm to the kitchen or the sunroom. All those silver baby spoons or rattles you have tucked away in a drawer would make a delightful wind chime for a daughter or niece. Small bells can be attached to the ends of these items to add more sounds, certain to catch the attention of anyone close by.

Many ordinary materials make attractive chimes. These can include seashells, antique keys, earrings or other jewelry pieces, for example.

This delicate wind chime not only makes dainty sounds, it is also a lovely addition to a kitchen, sunroom, or protected porch. Saltcellar spoons and crystal place-card holders are the chimes, a crystal drop from a chandelier is the center prism, and a silver-plated candy dish is the mounting plate. The suspension chain is cut from a silver necklace purchased for five dollars at a flea market. Decorative silver beads add interest and conceal glue points. Designed and constructed by Michael Kellett. Photograph by Jerry Koser.

Mounting plates should be selected that are of appropriate size and that suit the decorative style of the objects used as chimes. With silver items, a small candy dish works well. An ornate antique door plate would be an excellent choice for a wind chime of old keys, and a small piece of driftwood would work beautifully as a mounting plate for shells used as chimes. The tools and other items needed include a drill with a small bit, a wire cutter, glue, fishing line or delicate chain, various sizes of S-hooks, and whatever you want to use as a suspension chain.

Decorative wind chimes can find a place outdoors, as long as the materials used can withstand changes in weather. If not, they can add a personal touch to a special place within the home.

In constructing a wind chime, we take part in a centuries-old tradition, allowing playful spring breezes to fill our days with calming moments. Those "sweet consorted" sounds invite us all "unto the pleasant time."

Melissa Lester is a freelance writer living in Wetumpka, Alabama, with her husband and two sons. She contributes to a number of magazines and authored the book Giving for All It's Worth.

Theater of the Sun

Wayne B. Dayton

I kiss the sun good morning
And chase the dew away—
I follow the shape of shadows
As they begin to play.

I race the climbing sunshine
And time goes drifting by—
I ride the climbing rainbows
And tie them to the sky.

I feel the breath of evening
And draw the shade of gloom—
I watch the night returning
And wrestle with the moon.

I brush the stars with moonbeams
And light the evening sky—
I touch the edge of darkness
Where graceful fairies fly.

I paddle on waves of candles
That trail the Milky Way—
I climb the stairs of stardust
Where the darkness greets the day.

A cherry orchard near Maplewood in Door County, Wisconsin, brightens the landscape. Photograph by Darryl R. Beers.

Another April

Jesse Stuart

The way Mom had dressed Grandpa you'd think there was a heavy snow on the ground but there wasn't. April was here instead and the sun was shining on the green hills where the wild plums and the wild crab apples were in bloom enough to make you think there were big snowdrifts sprinkled over the green hills. "I'm a-goin' to see my old friend," Grandpa said just as Mom came down the stairs with his gloves.

"I'll be a-goin' to see 'im," Grandpa said to Mom. "I know he'll still be there."

And when Grandpa left the house I wanted to go with him, but Mom wouldn't let me go. I watched him as he walked slowly down the path in front of our house. Mom stood there watching Grandpa too. I think she was afraid that he would fall.

"He used to be a powerful man," Mom said more to herself than she did to me. "He was a timber cutter. No man could cut more timber than my father; no man in the timber woods could sink an ax deeper into a log than my father. And no man could lift the end of a bigger saw log than Pap could."

"Who is Grandpa goin' to see, Mom?" I asked.

"He's not goin' to see anybody," Mom said.

"I heard 'im say that he was goin' to see an old friend," I told her.

"Oh, he was just a-talkin'," Mom said.

"How long has Grandpa been with us?" I asked.

"Before you's born," she said. "Pap has been with us eleven years. He was eighty when he quit cuttin' timber and farmin'; now he's ninety-one."

As I watched Grandpa go down the path toward the hog pen he stopped to examine every little thing along his path. Once he waved his cane at a butterfly as it zigzagged over his head, its polkadot wings fanning the blue April air. When he reached the hog pen he called the hogs down to the fence. They came running and grunting to Grandpa just like they were talking to him. He leaned his cane against the hog pen, reached over the fence, and

Hardy crocuses bloom through a late winter snow. Photograph by William H. Johnson.

patted the hogs' heads. Grandpa didn't miss patting one of our seven hogs.

I knew that Grandpa loved the sunshine and the fresh April air that blew from the redbud and dogwood blossoms. He loved the bumblebees, the hogs, the pine cones, and pine needles. Grandpa didn't miss a thing along his walk. But each year he didn't take as long a walk as he had taken the year before. And when I could first remember Grandpa going on his walks he used to go out of sight. He'd go all over the farm. And he'd come to the house and take me on his knee and tell me about all that he had seen. Now Grandpa wasn't getting out of sight. We watched Grandpa as he walked down beside our smokehouse where a tall sassafras tree's thin leaves fluttered in the blue April wind. When Grandpa reached the smokehouse he leaned his cane against the sassafras tree. He let himself down slowly to his knees as he looked carefully at the ground. Grandpa was looking at something and I wondered what it was.

"There you are, my good old friend," Grandpa said.

"Who is his friend, Mom?" I asked.

Mom didn't say anything. Then I saw.

"He's playin' with that old terrapin, Mom."

"I know he is," Mom said. "The terrapin knows your Grandpa."

"My old friend, how do you like the sunshine?" Grandpa asked the terrapin.

The terrapin turned his fleshless face to one side like a hen does when she looks at you in the sunlight. He was trying to talk to Grandpa.

"Old fellow, it's been a hard winter," Grandpa said, "How have you fared under the smokehouse floor?"

"Does the terrapin know what Grandpa is sayin'?" I asked Mom.

"I don't know," she said.

"I'm awfully glad to see you, old fellow," Grandpa said.

"That terrapin has spent the winters under that smokehouse for fifteen years," Mom said. "Pap has been acquainted with him for eleven years. He's been talkin' to that terrapin every spring."

"How does Grandpa know the terrapin is old?" I asked Mom.

"It's got '1847' cut on its shell," Mom said. "We know he's ninety-five years old. We don't know how old he was when that date was cut on his back."

"Are you well, old fellow?" Grandpa asked the terrapin.

The terrapin just looked at Grandpa.

"I'm as well as common for a man of my age," Grandpa said. "Wait until the tomatoes get ripe and we'll go to the garden together."

"Does a terrapin eat tomatoes?" I asked Mom.

"Yes, that terrapin has been eatin' tomatoes from our garden for fifteen years," Mom said. "When Mick was tossin' the terrapins out of the tomato patch he picked up this one and found the date cut on his back. He put him back in the patch and told him to help himself. He lives from our garden every year. We don't bother him and don't allow anybody else to bother him. He spends his winters under our smokehouse floor buried in the dry ground."

"Gee, Grandpa looks like the terrapin," I said.

Mom didn't say anything; tears came to her eyes. She wiped them from her eyes with the corner of her apron.

"I'll be back to see you," Grandpa said. "I'm a-gettin' a little chilly; I'll be gettin' back to the house."

The terrapin poked his head deeper into the wind, holding one eye on Grandpa, for I could see his eye shining in the sinking sunlight.

Grandpa got his cane that was leaned against the sassafras tree trunk and hobbled slowly toward the house. The terrapin looked at him with first one eye and then the other.

I Like Rains
Ethel Plum

I like a rain that
gently patters,
softly chatters,
While its silver fingers play melodies
along my windowpane.

I love a rain that
swiftly rushes,
loudly gushes,
Across a parched, dry field
of growing grain.

I adore a rain that
dances lightly,
sparkles brightly,
On tree and grass and
mountain steep.

I cherish a rain that
has a song,
sings it long,
And lulls me off
to sleep. . . .

A Rainstorm
Buel B. Buzzard

I watched it rain last night; I heard the droplets fall,
Like a gentle benediction over plants and trees and all.
I saw the lightning flashing; I heard the thunder roar;
And they both spoke to me of things I hadn't thought before:
How each little raindrop was once a part of the tide
Until the wind and rain returned it to the mountainside,
Where each drop wrapped itself around a little grain of dust
And both returned to earth again to bless both it and us.
So, without the sandstorm we couldn't have the rain
To make forests green again and flowers to bloom on the plain.
"How like man," the thunder said, "how quickly he complains
If things don't go to please him, how soon he is to blame.
But I suppose it's ignorance which keeps him in that vein
Not knowing that good things will come to him only after rain."

A young boy enjoys the exuberant splatter of rain.
Photograph from Robertstock/Retrofile.

The Cataract of Lodore

Robert Southey

"How does the water
Come down at Lodore?"
From its sources which well
In the tarn on the fell;
From its fountains
In the mountains,
Its rills and its gills;
Through moss and through brake,
It runs and it creeps
For awhile, till it sleeps
In its own little lake.
And thence at departing,
Awakening and starting,
It runs through the reeds
And away it proceeds,
Through meadow and glade,
In sun and in shade,
And through the wood-shelter,
Among crags in its flurry,
Helter-skelter,
Hurry-scurry.
Here it comes sparkling,
And there it lies darkling;
Now smoking and frothing
Its tumult and wrath in,

Till in this rapid race
On which it is bent,
It reaches the place
Of its steep descent.

The cataract strong
Then plunges along,
Striking and raging
As if a war waging
Its caverns and rocks among:
Rising and leaping,
Sinking and creeping,
Swelling and sweeping,
Showering and springing,
Flying and flinging,
Writhing and ringing,
Eddying and whisking,
Spouting and frisking,
Turning and twisting,
Around and around
With endless rebound!
Smiting and fighting,
A sight to delight in;
Confounding, astounding,
Dizzying and deafening the ear with its sound.

And dashing and flashing and splashing and clashing;
And so never ending, but always descending,
Sounds and motions forever and ever are blending,
All at once and all o'er, with a mighty uproar;
And this way the water comes down at Lodore.

The waters of Proxy Falls, in Oregon, tumble down the hillside.
Photograph from Robertstock/Retrofile.

FOR THE CHILDREN

April Rain Song

Eileen Spinelli

Celebrate this rainy day.

Grab your raincoat. Splash away.

Croak like bullfrog. Quack like duck.

March through mud. (But don't get stuck!)

Ask a friend to join the fun.

Rain can be as sweet as sun.

Leap like lambs across the grass.

Count umbrellas as they pass.

Catch some drip-drops in a jar.

Scrub a scooter. Suds a car.

Sing an April shower song.

Robin just might sing along.

Puddles beckon. Come and play.

Celebrate this rainy day.

REMEMBER WHEN

Judy Lea

FOUR EASTER DRESSES

Spring has knocked on our door early this year, and I am taking the morning to carefully fold the family quilts and put them away in the guest-room closet. The one that touches my heart is the wedding-ring quilt my grandmother made for my mother, who in turn handed it down to me. Feeling its familiar softness, I remember the spring of 1952, the Easter of my sixth year.

In February, my mother and I had planned a trip from our home in Lebanon, Tennessee, to spend the weekend with my grandparents. My father, a pharmacist just like my grandfather, was scheduled to work through the weekend, along with my older brother, Ernie, who worked Saturdays behind the soda fountain. They were staying home.

Sitting in the front seat of the car was a rare treat for me. As Mother drove down the highway, I felt very regal and imagined that the Buick was a turquoise-and-white carriage pulled by high-stepping horses. Mother drove around the back of my grandparents' house to the basement garage and unpacked our white train cases and her hat box, but I could not wait. I ran up the back stairs, burst into the kitchen, and bounded onto Grandmother's lap.

After we placed freshly baked chocolate chip cookies on wire racks to cool, Grandmother invited me into her bedroom to see the Butterick pattern she had selected for my Easter dress. This year my grandmother had made special plans.

My Aunt Vivian, who was Mother's twin, and her family, including my cousin Alice Faye, were coming to visit Grandmother for Easter weekend; but they would drive to Lebanon on Sunday for our church service. Grandmother

---

This year my grandmother had made special plans.

---

had decided that she would make identical dresses for my mother, my aunt, my cousin, and me. She had selected a brown-and-white-checked cotton fabric that she believed would look very stylish with white cotton gloves and white leather pumps. The pattern had the new dropped waistline.

I tried to stand as still as possible, my toes curled inside my Buster Brown shoes, while she pinned thin paper pattern pieces against me. Grandmother said, "I declare, you must have grown five inches over the winter!" I had not, of course, but I always felt like standing taller and straighter and more princess-like when she said that.

By the time we got around to the last fitting, my excitement over the dresses had diminished. Since I had had each fitting twice, once for my dress and once for my cousin's, the new design and colors did not seem so special. When marking the

A young lady stands proudly as she is measured for a new dress.
Photograph by H. Armstrong Roberts, Robertstock/Retrofile.

The whole family sat together during the long church service. I did not whisper with Alice Faye during the sermon. I did not scribble notes on the offering envelopes or slip off my stiff white shoes. Instead, I sat thinking about Mother's words in Sunday School, about doing something difficult in order to help those you love. Grandmother had spent many hours making four dresses. Planning and sewing these dresses had taken most of her time the six weeks before Easter—Granddaddy had complained that she had forgotten he was in the house. Had I ever said "thank you"?

When I have a moment to think of my childhood, I remember that Easter Sunday with special fondness. It was a time when we all lived in a loving family and easily forgave each other our annoyances. It was also the first time I understood the meaning of sacrifice, both in my grandmother's example and, more importantly, in Christ's.

hem was the only chore left, Mother kneeled alongside Grandmother, held the yardstick, and cautioned me to "Be still." Grandmother, holding the pins in her mouth very carefully, would monotonously say "Turn" every few minutes. Invariably, I would lean on one foot more than the other and the hem would be uneven.

The four of us did turn heads that Easter Sunday morning at church. Mother was the superintendent of the Primary Department, so Alice Faye and I had to behave during the Bible storytime. We fidgeted until Mother brought out the felt board. As Mother placed each individual figure from the Gospel account of the Resurrection of Jesus onto the board, Alice Faye and I forgot what we were wearing and listened without stirring. Mother spoke of how hard it must have been for Mary to give up her Son. At the conclusion, she pulled off the gray felt "stone" signifying the open door to Christ's tomb.

There were other Easter dresses and other church services but none was as special as that one perfect Sunday. My grandmother never attempted this sewing feat again—she said she had seen brown and white checks in her dreams for months, and that once, proudly, was enough.

The memories of those dresses, Grandmother's love, and the Easter lesson my mother gave us are true gifts. The wedding-ring quilt now folded in my lap is my favorite and I handle it tenderly as I place it on the closet shelf. It is the one patiently sewn with so much love, with many small pieces of brown-and-white-checked cotton fabric.

Judy Lea is a registered perinatal nurse educator and lives with her husband, Jim, in Lebanon, Tennessee. They have three sons and a "precious" daughter-in-law. Cousin Alice Faye and her husband continue to visit often from Arkansas.

The Yellow Violet
William Cullen Bryant

When beechen buds begin to swell,
   And woods the bluebird's warble know,
The yellow violet's modest bell
   Peeps from the last year's leaves below.

Ere russet fields their green resume,
   Sweet flower, I love, in forest bare,
To meet thee, when thy faint perfume
   Alone is in the virgin air.

Of all her train, the hands of Spring
   First plant thee in the watery mould,
And I have seen thee blossoming
   Beside the snowbank's edges cold.

Thy parent sun, who bade thee view
   Pale skies, and chilling moisture sip,
Has bathed thee in his own bright hue,
   and streaked with jet thy glowing lip.

Yet slight thy form, and low thy seat,
   And earthward bent thy gentle eye,
Unapt the passing view to meet
   when loftier flowers are flaunting nigh.

Oft, in the sunless April day,
   Thy early smile has stayed my walk;
But midst the gorgeous blooms of May,
   I passed thee on thy humble stalk.

So they, who climb to wealth, forget
   The friends in darker fortunes tried.
I copied them—but I regret
   That I should ape the ways of pride.

And when again the genial hour
   Awakes the painted tribes of light,
I'll not o'erlook the modest flower
   That made the woods of April bright.

Trilliums!
Rachel Wallace-Oberle

I've walked these woods a thousand times
Through fragrant fir and pine
And thought my heart knew very well
Each sweetly curving swell;
Yet past the stream, just out of sight,
Winks a glimpse of white.
What promise waits? What grand affair?
What graceful glory there?
With quickened step through bough I wend
To find a ballet penned.

Trilliums! Trilliums! Everywhere!
Dancing beauties fair,
Saucy sprites made glad by sun
Bend and sway as one,
Swirling silken cloaks of cream
Across a ballroom green.
Trilliums! Trilliums! Fallen stars
Shining near and far,
Enchanting all who pass this way
With rhapsodies this warm spring day.

Large-flowered trilliums make a woodland spring carpet in Door County, Wisconsin. Photograph by Darryl R. Beers.

To a Rabbit Hurrying

Grace Cornell Tall

O little rabbit hurrying,
To your earth-nest scurrying
So fast you skim the ground,
    In the mirror of your eye
Did you see me? How you fly!
How your heart must pound.

Come back, I say.
Oh, can't you see
I am a friend? It's only *me*;
    Your fear's a false alarm.
    Not a whisker, not a hair
Of the new spring coat you wear
    Do I want to harm.

I'm only out to greet the spring,
And in the sun to dance and sing.
    Why must you run away?
    O little rabbit hurrying,
So full of needless worrying,
    I only want to play.

A young lady makes new friends in a painting,
ALICE IN WONDERLAND, *by Frederick Morgan.*
Fine Art Photographic Library Ltd., London.

READERS' FORUM

Snapshots from our IDEALS readers

Right: Gordon and Adeline Schmitz of Kiel, Wisconsin, spend Mondays baby-sitting their grandchildren, Liliana and Jacob. This photo of six-month-old Liliana was taken as a surprise Easter gift for her parents.

Below left: Lauren, six, and Kyle, four, are the children of Jeff and Malinda Ferrell of Knightdale, North Carolina. Their grandmother, Mrs. Evelyn Williams, also of Knightdale, poses them in front of her flower garden.

Below right: Eliza and Abigayle O'Neal, granddaughters of Howard and Peggie O'Neal of Irwin, Pennsylvania, are fascinated by their grandmother's daffodils. Mrs. Lucille Parry, also of Irwin, sends this photo of her great-grandchildren.

Above and right:
Grace Gibson of DeKalb,
Mississippi, sends us this photo of her granddaughter
Brittany, five, stretched out in her great-grandparents' daffodil
field. Another granddaughter, Carrie-Grace, two and a half,
holds her grandmother's dog, Keeley, who has just been found in
the clover field. Their parents are Shane and Elisa Baty, and
they are the great-granddaughters of Esther Smith.

Below: Special friends deserve beautiful flowers!
Three-year-olds Rachel, daughter of Drew and
Patti Martin of Wrightsville, Pennsylvania,
and Dylan, son of Dennis and Denise Haldeman
of Landisville, Pennsylvania, are great friends
as well as cousins.

A BIG "THANK YOU" to all who submitted
their precious photographs to *Ideals*. We
hope to hear from other readers who want
to share with the *Ideals* family. Please
include a self-addressed, stamped envelope
if you would like the photographs returned.
Or keep your originals for safekeeping and
send duplicates, along with all appropriate information such as your name,
address, and telephone number, the
full names and ages of the children pictured, as well as the full
names and addresses of immedi-
ate family members, to:

Readers' Forum
Ideals Publications
535 Metroplex Drive, Suite 250
Nashville, Tennessee 37211

ideals®

Publisher, Patricia A. Pingry
Editor, Marjorie Lloyd
Designer, Marisa Calvin
Copy Editor, Melinda Rathjen
Permissions Editor, Patsy Jay
Contributing Writers, Lansing Christman,
Pamela Kennedy, Lisa Ragan, Laurie Hunter,
Melissa Lester, Fran Morley, and Judy Lea

ACKNOWLEDGMENTS

BUTLER, EDITH SHAW. "The Resurrection and the Life." Used by permission of Nancy B. Truesdell. BUZZARD, BUEL B. "A Rainstorm." Used by permission of Louise A. Buzzard. FRANCK, INEZ. "At Easter Sunrise." Used by permission of Caroline R. Stevens. JAQUES, EDNA. "Dreamin'" from *The Golden Road,* published by Thomas Allen, Ltd., 1953. Used by permission of Louise Bonnell. RORKE, MARGARET L. "The Easter Message." Used by permission of Margaret A. Rorke. STUART, JESSE. An excerpt from "Another April." Copyright © 1942 by *Harper's Magazine.* Used by special permission. YOUNG, ALLEN M. An excerpt from *Small Creatures and Ordinary Places* by Allen M. Young. Reprinted courtesy of The University of Wisconsin Press. Our sincere thanks to the following, whom we were unable to locate: Geneva Davies for "Spring Sang to Me"; The Estate of Mary E. McCullough for "Easter Theme"; The Estate of Raphael Harwood Miller for a quote from "Good Morning! Christ Is Risen"; Eliot Porter for "Morning Dew" from *The Heart Has Its Seasons;* Tessa Sweazy Webb for "Responsive Heart."

Brooke Honnette is a source of "joy and delight" to her ninety-seven-year-old great-great-grandmother, Dorothy Crysler, Modesto, California. She is the one-year-old daughter of Richard and Cyndi Honnette of Sacramento, California.

STATEMENT OF OWNERSHIP, MANAGEMENT AND CIRCULATION (REQUIRED BY FORM 3526)
1. Publication Title: Ideals. 2. Publication Number: 0019-137X. 3. Filing Date: August 21, 2003. 4. Issue Frequency: 6. 5. Number of Issues Published Annually: 6. 6. Annual Subscription Price: $19.95. 7. Office of publication: Guideposts, A Church Corporation, 39 Seminary Hill Road, Carmel, NY 10512. 8. Location of headquarters: Guideposts, A Church Corporation, 39 Seminary Hill Road, Carmel, NY 10512. 9. The names and addresses of the publisher and the editor-in-chief are: Patricia A. Pingry, Ideals Publications, A Division of Guideposts, 535 Metroplex Dr., Ste. 250, Nashville, TN 37211; Editor: Michelle Prater Burke (same as publisher); Managing Editor: Michelle Prater Burke (same as publisher). 10. Owner: Guideposts, A Church Corporation, a New York not for-profit corporation, 39 Seminary Hill Road, Carmel, NY 10512. Names and addresses of individual owners; None. 11. The known bondholders, mortgagees, and other security holders owning or holding one percent or more of total amount of bonds, mortgages or other securities: None. 12. The exempt status has not changed during preceding 12 months. 13. Publication Name: Ideals. 14. Issue Date for Circulation Data: Thanksgiving '02 thru Friendship '03. 15. Average number of copies each issue during preceding twelve months: a. total number of copies printed: 148,359; b. (1) paid and/or requested circulation through outside-county mail subscriptions: 101,277; (2) paid and/or requested circulation through in-county subscriptions: None; (3) paid and/or requested circulation through dealer sales: 21,227; (4) paid and/or requested circulation through other classes: None; c.total paid and/or requested circulation: 122,503. d. (1) free distribution by mail through outside-county: 862; (2) free distribution by mail through in-county: None; (3) free distribution by mail through other classes: None; e. free distribution outside the mail: None; f. total free distribution: 7,375; g. total distribution: 129,879; h. copies not distributed: 18,480; i. total: 148,359. Percent Paid and/or requested circulation: 94.3%. Actual number of copies of single issue published nearest to filing date: 15.a. total number of copies printed: 129,219; b. (1) paid and/or requested circulation through outside-county mail subscriptions: 110,599; (2) paid and/or requested circulation through in-county subscriptions: None; (3) paid and/or requested circulation through dealer sales: 4352; (4) paid and/or requested circulation through other classes: None; c. total paid and/or requested circulation: 114,951; d. (1) free distribution by mail through outside-county: 1,000; (2) free distribution by mail through in-county: None; (3) free distribution by mail through other classes: None; e. free distribution outside the mail: None; f. total free distribution: 1,000; g. total distribution: 115,951; h. copies not distributed: 13,268; i. total: 129,219. Percent Paid and/or requested circulation: 99.1% 16. this Statement of Ownership will be printed in the Easter '04 issue of this publication. 17. I certify that the statements made to me above are correct and complete. Signed John F. Temple, President.

BENEATH THE CROSS...
The Stories of Those Who Stood at the Cross of Jesus

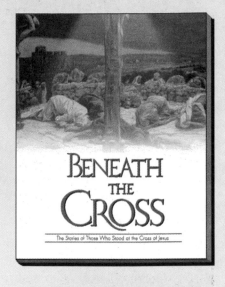

BENEATH THE CROSS follows the lives of those people who were with Jesus at the end of His life. Through Scriptures, poetry and prose, explore the lives of Mary, His Mother, the disciples and many others before they met Jesus, their relationships with Him, and their lives after His resurrection.

As you read through the pages of this dynamic book, you will feel the blessings, the joy, the sadness and the pain as those that loved and knew Him recount the days that lead to His death on the cross. But the cross was not the end, it was just the beginning.

This is the perfect book for the Easter season—the celebration of life everlasting and for all year round—it is a reminder of our Savior and His love for us.

Exclusive highlights—

- ✝ 160 Pages, heavy-weight enamel
- ✝ Full-color photographs of the Holy Lands
- ✝ Masterful paintings depicting the life of Jesus
- ✝ Scripture references

Your free gift just for ordering!

Complete the Free Examination Certificate and mail today for your 21-Day Preview. And receive a FREE *Easter Blessings* booklet just for ordering.

No need to send money now!

FREE EXAMINATION CERTIFICATE

YES! I'd like to examine **BENEATH THE CROSS** for 21 days FREE. If after 21 days I am not delighted with it, I may return it and owe nothing. If I decide to keep it, I will be billed $24.95, plus postage and handling. In either case, the FREE *Easter Blessings* booklet is mine to keep.

Total copies ordered _____

Please print your name and address:

_____
NAME

_____
ADDRESS   APT#

_____
CITY   STATE   ZIP

Allow 4 weeks for delivery. Orders subject to credit approval.
Send no money now. We will bill you later.
www.IdealsBooks.com   15/202171068

BUSINESS REPLY MAIL
FIRST-CLASS MAIL PERMIT NO. 38 CARMEL NY
POSTAGE WILL BE PAID BY ADDRESSEE

**NO POSTAGE
NECESSARY
IF MAILED
IN THE
UNITED STATES**

**GUIDEPOSTS
PO BOX 797
CARMEL NY 10512-9905**

God's Word Wasn't Written Just for Ministers, Kings and Scholars... it was meant... for Everyday People Like You and Me

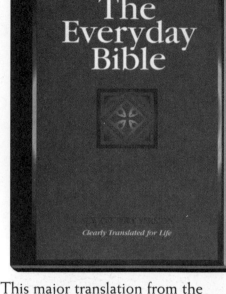

"Those who hear the teaching of God and obey it—they are the ones who are truly blessed." Luke 11:28 (TEB)

Recapture the freshness and spirit of God's Word as it was intended to be read...in the language of ordinary people! Find rich new meaning and clarity in every verse of **The Everyday Bible**...the easiest-to-read Bible translated ever!

Here is a perfect Bible, not only for beginners, but for everyone who loves God's Word. A Bible that gives you exciting "fresh looks" at passages you've known and loved for years!

This major translation from the original Hebrew and Greek Scripture text is far easier to read than other modern language Bibles, because the translators have sought specifically to preserve the Bible's "common man" approach.

Not a paraphrased, not an "abridged" Bible, but a major translation featuring:

- ✤ Updated terms and sentence structure
- ✤ Easy-to-read on page footnotes
- ✤ Large 10-point type and readable 2-column format
- ✤ Dictionary and Topical Concordance
- ✤ Eight color maps
- ✤ Convenient 6" x 8 ⅞" size—1,168 pages
- ✤ PLUS...a special devotional reading guide to lead you through the Bible subject by subject!

Your exclusive Guideposts price for this important Bible translation is

Only $18.96

payable in two installments of $9.48 each, plus postage and handling.
You save over 20% off the publisher's price.

FREE EXAMINATION CERTIFICATE

YES! I'd like to examine *The Everyday Bible* at no risk or obligation. If I decide to keep the book, I will be billed later at the low Guideposts price of only $18.96, payable in 2 installments of $9.48 each, plus postage and handling. If not completely satisfied, I may return the book within 30 days and owe nothing.

Total copies ordered: _____

Please print your name and address:

_____
NAME

_____
ADDRESS   APT#

_____
CITY   STATE   ZIP

Allow 4 weeks for delivery. Orders subject to credit approval.
Send no money now. We will bill you later.
www.guidepostsbooks.com

Printed in USA
11/202171094

Complete the Free Examination Certificate and mail today for your 30-Day Preview.

No need to send money now!